Dream Big

Published in 2023 by OH!
An imprint of Welbeck Non-Fiction Limited, part of Welbeck Publishing
Group. Offices in London, 20 Mortimer Street, London W1T 3JW, and
Sydney, 205 Commonwealth Street, Surry Hills 2010.
www.welbeckpublishing.com

A CIP catalogue record for this book is available from the British Library.

ISBN 978-1-83861-181-1

Publisher: Lisa Dyer
Compilation and writing: Katie Hewett
Design: Lucy Palmer
Production: Felicity Awdry

Printed and bound in Dubai

10 9 8 7 6 5 4 3 2 1

Dream Big

Inspirational Quotes for Brave Women

CONTENTS

INTRODUCTION

Embarking on new challenges, whether it's an education or career step, a business or side hustle, or a new city or country to live in, can be exhilarating and terrifying in equal measure. Along with the excitement and hope, there can often be self-doubt and fear. This book has been created to help you fulfil your biggest ambitions, and not let the practical matters of life derail your dreams.

A collection of positive, empowering and confidence-building quotes, sayings and advice from other women, who have been through setbacks and victories, *Dream Big* helps you aim for the stars, especially in those moments when you need an extra boost.

The first chapter, Reach for the Stars, encourages you to have the confidence to believe in yourself and your goals and to go for them. Seize the Day focuses on maximizing and creating opportunities, as well as finding the persistence and motivation to continue on your path. Find Your Tribe is about the amazing people you may meet along the way and how they can inform and enrich your experience.

The fourth chapter, Authentically You, reminds you to take the time to love and appreciate the person you are, to match your dreams to your values, and to determine what success means to you, and you alone.

Finally, Enjoy the Ride gives advice on how to navigate setbacks and obstacles, knowing that these are stepping stones to greater self-discovery, and to enjoy the journey.

Never forget to give yourself a standing ovation for your achievements, no matter how small. Reward yourself for the positives every day and ...

DREAM BIG.

REACH FOR
THE STARS

You can do anything you set your mind to; don't let anyone tell you otherwise. Set your goals, visualize your achievements, take risks and make your dreams reality. Have self-belief, lean into ambition and don't lowball your aspirations.

" The future belongs to those who BELIEVE in the BEAUTY of their DREAMS. "

Eleanor Roosevelt,
former First Lady of the USA

66

Every great dream begins with a dreamer. Always remember, you have within you the strength, the patience and the passion to reach for the stars to change the world.

99

Harriet Tubman, social activist

Take your risks now. As you grow older, you become more fearful and less flexible ... Try to keep your mind open to possibilities and your mouth closed on matters that you don't know about. Limit your "always" and your "nevers". Continue to share your heart with people even if it's been broken.

Amy Poehler, actor and comedian,
Harvard University speech, 2011

LITTLE GIRLS
with *Dreams*
BECOME

WOMEN
with *Vision*

" You and you alone are the only person who can live the life that writes the story that you were meant to tell. "

Kerry Washington, actor,
George Washington University speech, 2013

My favourite animal is the turtle. The reason is that in order for the turtle to move, it has to stick its neck out. There are going to be times in your life when you're going to have to stick your neck out. There will be challenges, and instead of hiding in a shell, you have to go out and meet them.

Ruth Westheimer,
sex therapist and talk-show host,
Trinity College speech, 2004

"

*You cannot dream
of becoming something
you do not know about.
You have to learn to*

dream big.

"

Sonia Sotomayor, lawyer,
Manhattan College speech, 2019

"

THE DREAM IS REAL

my friends.

The failure to realize it

is the only unreality.

"

Toni Cade Bambara,
author and social activist

SETTING GOALS

Make your dreams a reality by identifying your objective and setting out ways to achieve it.

1 Write down your goals – no matter how fanciful, outlandish or impossible they seem. Go for the max! This is about inspiration and manifesting the dream by seeing it written down, which makes it more real and tangible.

2 Visualize the goal. Imagine what it feels and looks like to have reached your goal. What is your life like? Describe it in detail.

3 Break it down. What are the steps that you need to get to that goal? Making lots of small goals over a long period is much less frightening and much more achievable than huge milestones that seem unlikely if not impossible from the start.

4 Consistently move towards your goal. Try not to give it 1000 per cent one day and then let it ride for a month. Small consistent steps win the race

5 Reward yourself for your mini-goals. Consistently congratulate yourself on your successes.

6 Remind yourself of the reasons you are on this path and the benefits you will get from attaining your goal.

7 Stay mentally positive and motivated. Surround yourself with positive people and stay clear of the Debbie Downers.

8 Focus. Don't allow distractions to derail you, or other more minor goals to get in the way.

If you want to run for Prime Minister, you can. If you don't, that's wonderful, too. Shave your armpits, don't shave them, wear flats one day, heels the next. These things are so irrelevant and surface to what it is all really about, and I wish people wouldn't get caught up in that. We want to empower women to do exactly what they want, to be true to themselves, to have the opportunities to develop.

Emma Watson, actor,
Elle magazine, 2014

Without leaps of imagination or dreaming, we lose the excitement of possibilities. Dreaming, after all, is a form of planning.

Gloria Steinem,
journalist and activist

BE BOLD.

Envision yourself living a life that you love. Believe, even if you can only muster your faith for just this moment, believe that the sort of life you wish to live is, at this very moment, just waiting for you to summon it up. And when you wish for it, you begin moving toward it, and it, in turn, begins moving toward you.

Suzan-Lori Parks,
playwright, novelist and musician,
Mount Holyoke College speech, 2001

• IT'S •
NEVER TOO LATE
TO FOCUS
ON YOUR
Dreams

> "
>
> When you have a dream, you've got to grab it and never let go.
>
> "

Carol Burnett, author and actor

"

Dreams
come a size
TOO BIG
so we can
GROW
into them.

"

Josie Bissett, actor

I would say to always follow your dream. And dream big because my whole career, including any of the things that I've accomplished, I never thought in a million years that I would be here. So, it just proves that once you believe in yourself, and you put your mind to something,

YOU CAN DO IT.

Simone Biles, gymnast

"

ALL DREAMS ARE WITHIN REACH.

All you have to do is keep moving towards them.

Honda "Yearbook" commercial, 2017

"

*When your dreams are bigger
than the places you find yourself in,
sometimes you need to seek out your
own reminders that there is more.
And there is always more waiting
for you on the other side of fear.*

"

Elaine Welteroth, journalist and TV host,
More Than Enough (2018)

"

Dreams don't have to just be dreams. You can make it a reality; if you just keep pushing and keep trying, then eventually you'll REACH YOUR GOAL.

"

Naomi Osaka, tennis player

"

Always keep your eyes open. Keep watching. Because whatever you see can INSPIRE YOU.

"

Grace Coddington, fashion editor

66

... no matter where you're from your dreams are valid.

99

Lupita Nyong'o, actor

> **"** If it doesn't scare you, you're probably not dreaming big enough. **"**
>
> Tory Burch, fashion designer

66

I always did something I was a little not ready to do . . . you push through those moments, that's when you have a BREAKTHROUGH.

99

Marissa Mayer, businesswoman, investor and former CEO of Yahoo!

"

DON'T LIMIT YOURSELF.

Many people limit themselves to what they think they can do. You can go as far as your mind lets you. What you believe, remember, you can achieve.

"

Mary Kay Ash,
founder of Mary Kay Cosmetics

"

GET INFORMED.
GET OUTRAGED.
GET INSPIRED.
GET ACTIVE.

"

Anita Roddick,
founder of The Body Shop

THE DISTANCE BETWEEN DREAMS AND REALITY IS CALLED ACTION

66

If you have a dream, don't just sit there. Gather courage to believe that you can succeed and leave no stone unturned to make it a reality.

99

Dr Roopleen Prasad, author of *Principles of Success Made Easy* (2017)

"

I've learnt that no one is too small to make a difference.

"

Greta Thunberg,
environmental activist

"

Be faithful to your dreams.

"

Tracey Emin, artist,
Embroidered handkerchief for Momart (1999)

"

You don't have to
change who you are
for anyone: if you are
your regular, authentic,
confident self, then you
can push to do whatever
you want.

"

Marsai Martin, actor

"

Don't be afraid to speak up for yourself. Keep fighting for your dreams!

"

Gabby Douglas, gymnast

MANAGE YOUR FEAR

Don't live a fear-based life. As we grow older, we question our behavior more, second guess, and worry about failing publicly. And with that, we lose the power to chase our dreams or take the plunge. Your life is your message, so don't let it be ruled by fear. Challenge yourself to always make the choice that you truly want, show the world why you are here, and never allow fear to be the reason you don't.

Antonia Hock,
Women on TOPP, August 2022

Give yourself permission to dream big. So often the limitations that we see are in our own minds and as women, we have been taught to aspire for less, to be "pleasing and grateful." This is the biggest impediment to success. Allow yourself to claim what you really want and then go for it!

Julia Haart,
director of Elite Model World,
Women on TOPP, August 2022

DON'T TALK, ACT.
DON'T SAY, DO.
DON'T PROMISE, PROVE.

*A heart
without dreams
is like a bird
without feathers.*

Suzy Kassem, author,
Rise Up and Salute the Sun
(2010)

To fulfil a dream, to be allowed to sweat over lonely labor, to be given a chance to create, is the meat and potatoes of life. The money is the gravy. As everyone else, I love to dunk my crust in it. But alone, it is not a diet designed to keep body and soul together.

Bette Davis, actor,
The Lonely Life: An Autobiography
(1962)

"

At the end of the day, you are the only one that is limiting your ability to dream, or to actually execute on your dreams. Don't let yourself get in the way of that.

"

Falon Fatemi, CEO of Fireside and Node

"

Excellence

is the best deterrent to

racism or sexism.

"

Oprah Winfrey

SEIZE
THE DAY

Working towards your dreams is about seeking out opportunities and taking those that come your way. If your dream job, lifestyle or personal goal feels out of reach, don't be afraid to go for it and give it all you have.

There is nothing more beautiful than finding your course as you believe you bob aimlessly in the current. Wouldn't you know that your path was there all along, waiting for you to knock, waiting for you to become. This path does not belong to your parents, your teachers, your leaders, or your lovers. Your path is your character defining itself more and more everyday like a photograph coming into focus.

Jodie Foster, actor,
University of Pennsylvania speech (2006)

"

The only thing you can do in this life is pursue your passions, celebrate your bloopers, and never stop following your fear.

"

Grace Helbig, comedian
Ramapo College speech, 2015

"

I didn't get there by wishing for it or hoping for it, but by

WORKING FOR IT.

"

Estée Lauder,
cosmetics founder and businesswoman

I have learned over the years that when one's mind is made up, this diminishes fear.

Rosa Parks, activist

Stay positive.
positive.
WORK HARD.

Make it
happen.

For every door that's been opened to me, I've tried to open my door to others ... Maybe then we can begin to fear less, to make fewer wrong assumptions, to let go of the biases and stereotypes that unnecessarily divide us ... It's not about being perfect. It's not about where you get yourself in the end. There's power in allowing yourself to be known and heard, in owning your unique story, in using your authentic voice. And there's grace in being willing to know and hear others. This, for me, is how we become.

Michelle Obama,
former First Lady of the USA,
Becoming (2018)

The most difficult thing is the decision to act, the rest is merely tenacity. The fears are paper tigers. You can do anything you decide to do. You can act to change and control your life; and the procedure, the process is its own reward.

Amelia Earhart, aviation pioneer

Sometimes we can only find our true direction when we let the wind of change carry us.

Mimi Novic,
motivational speaker

"

Life has got all those twists and turns. You've got to hold on tight and off you go.

"

Nicole Kidman, actor

No, this is not the beginning of a new chapter in my life; this is the beginning of a new book! That first book is already closed, ended, and tossed into the seas; this new book is newly opened, has just begun!

Look, it is the first page! And it is a beautiful one!

C. JoyBell C., author

"

I want every little girl who's told she's bossy to be told instead she has leadership skills.

"

Sheryl Sandberg,
businesswoman and philanthropist

"

*The most common way
people give up their
power is by thinking
they don't have any.*

"

Alice Walker, author

Work hard for what you want because it won't come to you without a fight. You have to be strong and courageous and know that you can do anything you put your mind to. If somebody puts you down or criticizes you, just keep on believing in yourself and turn it into something positive.

Leah LaBelle, singer

66

> If you push through that feeling of being scared, that feeling of taking risk, really amazing things can happen.

Marissa Mayer,
businesswoman, investor and
former CEO of Yahoo!

BUILD YOUR CONFIDENCE

One of the biggest reasons follow-through doesn't happen when opportunities are presented is a lack of self-confidence. No one is entirely ready for their next challenge – that's why it's a challenge. Everyone to some degree is making it up as they go!

1 Don't undervalue your ideas or time – your contribution is just as important as anyone else's. You are worthy!

2 Avoid apologizing or undermining yourself. Look out for words like "sorry", "just", "I'm not" in your emails, texts, posts and the words you say in conversations.

3 Be physically confident or fake it until you make it. Enter a room confidently, stand up straight and be aware of your body language.

4 Think like an Olympic athlete and train by accumulating small wins to build confidence. The big wins will follow.

5 Have faith, positivity and keep moving. Bring your energy to the game.

"I felt like it was time to set up my future, SO I SET A GOAL. My goal was INDEPENDENCE."

Beyoncé Knowles,
singer-songwriter and actor

"

Whatever the problem, be part of the solution. Don't just sit around raising questions and pointing out obstacles.

"

Tina Fey, actor, comedian and author,
Bossypants (2011)

"

Tomorrow is the beginning of your

ANYTHING.

"

Lizzo, singer,
Twitter, 2019

Sometimes the smallest step in the right direction ends up being the biggest step of your life.

SPOTTING OPPORTUNITIES

1. **Be Observant:** Pay attention, be curious and look around you at the situations and ideas that are being discussed. Schedule time outside of work or distractions to expose yourself to new experiences.

2. **Educate Yourself:** Research your objectives—get to know everything you can about them and how to achieve them. Become an expert in your area. Seek out information from others who have gone down the same road, grow your network of contacts and find a mentor.

3. **Know Yourself:** Your skills, strengths and values will give you clues as to the direction opportunities may lie. If you're having trouble focusing on one path, ask yourself if it feels authentic to you.

4. **Be Persistent:** The most successful are not always the most talented. Be committed and work hard. Leave no stone unturned.

5. **Be Flexible:** Consider change and roll with the unexpected.

66

Persistence proves to the person you're trying to reach that you're passionate about something, that you really want something.

99

Norah O'Donnell,
television journalist for NBC and CBS

"

Nothing is going to
be handed to you.
You have to make
things happen.

"

Florence Griffith-Joyner, athlete

Failure only truly exists in being too scared to ever try at all, in my opinion. Be willing to fail, be willing to fall, be open to critique and alteration; be ready for it to be public sometimes. Be prepared for the growing pains, and be grateful for the abundance of new information and for the journey of progress.

Jameela Jamil, actor and presenter, *Teen Vogue* Commencement, 2020

"

OPPORTUNITIES

are usually disguised
as hard work,
so most people
don't recognize them.

"

Ann Landers, columnist

IF
OPPORTUNITY
DOESN'T KNOCK,
BUILD A DOOR

> **66**
>
> **I think the truth of the matter is, people who end up as 'first' don't actually set out to be first. They set out to do something they love, and it just so happens that they are the**
>
> # FIRST TO DO IT.
>
> **99**

Condoleezza Rice,
former US Secretary of State

Find out what you like doing best and get somebody to pay you for doing it.

Katharine Whitehorn,
journalist

You get in life
what you have
the courage
to ask for.

Oprah Winfrey

Rarely are opportunities presented to you in a perfect way. In a nice little box with a yellow bow on top. "Here, open it, it's perfect. You'll love it." Opportunities – the good ones – are messy, confusing and hard to recognize.

THEY'RE RISKY.
THEY CHALLENGE YOU.

Susan Wojcicki, CEO of YouTube

FIND
YOUR TRIBE

No woman is an island. To achieve your dreams you need your support system, whether that's family, friends, colleagues or a business network. Build alliances and make yourself stronger by seeking out and championing other women. Listening to the advice and ideas of female leaders will help motivate and inspire you.

What I want young women and girls to know is: You are powerful and your voice matters. You're going to walk into many rooms in your life and career where you may be the only one who looks like you or who has had the experiences you've had. But you remember that when you are in those rooms, you are not alone. We are all in that room with you applauding you on. Cheering your voice. And just so proud of you. So, you use that voice

AND BE STRONG.

Kamala Harris, *Vice President of the USA*

"

Call it a clan, call it a network, call it a tribe, call it a family: Whatever you call it, whoever you are, you need one.

"

Jane Howard, author,
Families (1978)

> ## 66
>
> *We're here for a reason. I believe a bit of the reason is to throw little torches out to lead people through the dark.*
>
> ## 99

Whoopi Goldberg,
actor and talk-show host

The worst thing that we can do as women is not stand up for each other, and this is something we can practise every day, no matter where we are and what we do – women sticking up for other women, choosing to protect and celebrate each other instead of competing or criticising one another.

Amal Clooney, human rights lawyer

When you respect the idea that you are sharing the Earth with other humans, and when you lead with your nice foot forward, you'll win, every time. It might not be today, it might not be tomorrow, but it comes back to you when you need it.

Kristen Bell, actor,
USC School of Dramatic Arts speech, 2019

66

*We meet
the people we're
supposed to
when the time
is just right.*

99

Alyson Noël, author

MIND MAP YOUR NETWORK

Here's a tip from the Center of Creative Leadership.

On a piece of paper draw your name in a circle and write down the names of people with whom you have strong connections — put them close to the circle. Write the names of those with whom you have more distant ties farther away from the circle. Finally, ask yourself who should be in your network that isn't. Place them (either by name or role) farthest out on your paper.

Look for patterns and analyze the types of relationships these are. You may have strong emotional support but weaker career support. How could you build relationships that support your weaker areas?

DON'T LET
Anyone
STEAL YOUR DREAM.
IT'S YOUR
DREAM
NOT THEIRS.

"

Networking is not about just connecting people. It's about connecting people with people, people with ideas, and people with OPPORTUNITIES.

"

Michele Jennae, author,
The Connectworker (2013)

66

Women's networks are a necessary part of life ... a mixture of empathy and brainstorming can move mountains.

99

Hazel Hawke, author and advocate

"

I've always believed that one woman's success can only help another woman's success.

"

Gloria Vanderbilt,
author and fashion designer

*Motivation comes from
working on things we care about.
It also comes from working
with people we care about.*

Sheryl Sandberg,
entrepreneur

We're connected, as women. It's like a spiderweb. If one part of that web vibrates, if there's trouble, we all know it, but most of the time we're just too scared, or selfish, or insecure to help. But if we don't help each other, who will?

Sarah Addison Allen, author

"

Do not follow where the path may lead. Go instead where there is no path and leave a trail.

"

Muriel Strode, poet

KEEP THE DRAWBRIDGE DOWN

When you reach the most senior of positions – the C-suite or board level – keep the drawbridge down. Walk down it, stand beside the woman at its base and walk back up with her to where you are, and cheer her on as she advances beyond you. Open doors for her, whether she's aware of it or not, and without condition – knowing in your own heart that her success is a product of yours. Then sit back and enjoy the multiplier effect.

**Yetunde Hofmann,
founder of SOLARIS**

"

I am strong enough to make others believe in their dreams again.

"

Yusra Mardini,
Syrian refugee and Olympian swimmer

HEPEATED:

WHEN A WOMAN SUGGESTS AN IDEA AND IT'S IGNORED, BUT THEN A MAN SAYS THE SAME THING AND EVERYONE THINKS IT IS A STROKE OF GENIUS

HELPING WOMEN RISE

When progressing towards your dreams, take a hand from other women and give a hand. Here is some advice from Janice Sutherland, a women's leadership expert and founder of This Woman Can, on LinkedIn, in February 2020.

1. **Celebrate the Difference:** Respect the talents of other women in your company and bolster their reputation within the workplace.

2. **Be Honest:** Praise women's achievements of course, but you are doing a disservice if you only tell them half the story. Don't be afraid to give or receive constructive comments on how you can improve.

3. **Collaborate not Separate:** Jump in to give help where it's needed and support rather than compete. There's plenty of room for all of us at the top.

4. **Advocate:** Give a shout-out to other women's achievements and ideas.

5. **Share the Love:** Welcome women into the fold and include them in opportunities whenever you can. Be on the lookout for opportunities that may suit them.

... We need to speak up, sit in the first row at important meetings, mutually support each other and emphasize the importance of collaborating rather than competing against each other. We may not be liked for doing so, but we will slowly gain the respect and attention we deserve.

Marianna Zangrillo,
corporate leader and investor

SAY NO!

I KNOW SO MANY PHENOMENAL WOMEN WHO STRUGGLE DAILY WITH THIS INABILITY TO SAY NO – TAKING ON TOO MUCH AND NEGLECTING THEMSELVES. SO FROM ONE FEMALE LEADER TO ANOTHER, WE NEED TO TELL EACH OTHER IN NO UNCERTAIN TERMS THAT IT IS OKAY TO PUT THE BRAKES ON AND JUST SAY NO!

Jessica Robinson,
author of *Financial Feminism*

Make your vision
so clear that
your fears
become irrelevant

66

A good leader is able to paint a picture of a vision for the future and then enlist others to go on the journey with her. A truly conscious leader recognizes that it is not about her, but that the team is looking to her for inspiration and direction. Keeping her ego in check is essential.

99

Tamra Ryan,
CEO of Women's Bean Project

66

You need to spend political capital - be unafraid to introduce people, compliment somebody when it's deserved and stand up for something you really believe in, rather than just go with the flow.

99

Amy Schulman,
partner at Polaris Partners

If you don't have
a vision, you're going
to be stuck in what you
know. And the only
thing you know is what
you've already seen.

Iyanla Vanzant, inspirational speaker

AUTHENTICALLY YOU

Knowing your authentic self will not only help you create and realize your dreams, and work towards them, but also help you develop your unique version of the kind of success that brings you happiness.

66

If you always do what interests you, at least one person is pleased.

99

Katharine Hepburn, actor

"

There is always going to be a reason why you can't do something; your job is to constantly look for the reasons why you can achieve your dreams.

"

Shannon Miller, gymnast

66

The most significant successes come from letting your light shine, embracing failure, and getting good at being wrong.

99

Stacey Abrams, politician

Just believe in yourself. Even if you don't, pretend that you do and, at some point, you will.

**Venus Williams,
tennis player**

"

Opportunities are often things you haven't noticed the first time around.

"

Catherine Deneuve, actor

"

Keep your dreams alive.
Understand to achieve anything
requires faith and belief in
yourself, vision, hard work,
determination and dedication.
Remember all things are possible
for those who believe.

"

Gail Devers, track and field sprinter

"

Define success on your own terms, achieve it by your own rules, and build a life you're proud to live.

"

Anne Sweeney,
former president of Disney ABC

66

Every time you suppress some part of yourself or allow others to play you small, you are in essence ignoring the owner's manual your creator gave you and destroying your design.

99

Oprah Winfrey,
O magazine, February 2003

DREAM BIG

start small
BUT most of all

START

66

**A leader takes people
where they want to go.
A GREAT LEADER
takes people where they don't
necessarily want to go, but
ought to be.**

99

Rosalynn Carter,
former First Lady of the USA

Sometimes your insecurities and your inexperience may lead you, too, to embrace other people's expectations, standards or values. But you can harness that inexperience to carve out your own path, one that is free of the burden of knowing how things are supposed to be. A path that is defined by its own particular set of reasons.

Natalie Portman, actor

"

**Don't ever doubt
yourselves or waste a
second of your life.
It's too short and
you're too special.**

"

Ariana Grande, singer

"

We do not need

MAGIC

to change the world, we carry all the POWER we need inside ourselves already: we have the

power to imagine better.

"

J. K. Rowling, author

66

It's your turn to choose
and define what success
means to you. Now,
others will try to define it
for you, but yours is the
only voice that matters.

99

Octavia Spencer, actor

People who

SHINE

FROM WITHIN
don't need
A SPOTLIGHT

BELIEVE AND BE YOU.
Be unique.

Be prepared to be alone sometimes when you're unique. It's not a bad thing. You could travel with the sheep, follow everybody else's stuff but then you're not you. I guess if I want to say anything it's "Be you." Be true to you and that should make the ride a little

MORE INTERESTING.

Whoopi Goldberg, actor and talk-show host

"

Don't you ever
let a soul in the
world tell you
that you can't be
exactly who you are.

"

Lady Gaga, singer-songwriter

66

Always be the first-rate version of yourself, instead of the second-rate version of somebody else.

99

Judy Garland, actor

"

When I was a little girl and my teachers sent notes home complaining that I was as loud as the boys, that it wasn't ladylike for a girl to be this outspoken, this raucous, instead of forcing me to tone it down ... [you] told me to use my voice by shouting to my heart's content, told me never to forget that I was a girl not a mouse and if I believed I had to change myself to suit anyone else I shouldn't, that no matter what they said my voice was so important.

"

Nikita Gill, writer

It takes a lot for you
to find your confidence,
but you shouldn't let
someone else be the
person to find it for you.

Justine Skye, singer

> **"**
> *A girl should be two things: who and what she wants.*
> **"**

Coco Chanel, fashion designer

Always be yourself because if you're not yourself, who are you? Someone else, therefore not being you at all.

Luna Lovegood,
Harry Potter and the Order of the Phoenix

66

A wise girl knows her limits; a smart girl knows that she has none.

99

Marilyn Monroe, actor

> **66**
>
> ... character – the willingness to accept responsibility for one's own life – is the source from which self-respect springs.
>
> **99**

Joan Didion, writer

"

There is a fountain of youth: it is your mind, your talents, the creativity you bring to your life and the lives of the people you love.

"

Sophia Loren, actor

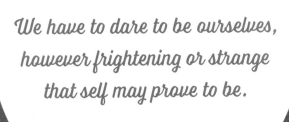

*We have to dare to be ourselves,
however frightening or strange
that self may prove to be.*

May Sarton, poet

"

IT NEEDS TO BE SAID AND HEARD: IT'S OKAY TO BE WHO YOU ARE.

"

Hailee Steinfeld, actor

"

My mother told me to be a lady. And for her, that meant to be your own person, be independent.

"

Ruth Bader Ginsburg, lawyer

"

Don't compromise yourself. You are all you've got.

"

Janis Joplin,
singer and musician

"

What makes you different or weird – that is your strength.

"

Meryl Streep, actor

"

The only person I really believe in is ME.

"

Debbie Harry, singer

"

Just enjoy every moment – don't stress. Just be yourself.

"

Mabel, singer

Since I don't look like
every other girl, it takes
a while to be okay with that.

To be different.
BUT DIFFERENT
IS GOOD.

Serena Williams,
tennis player

66

Whatever your truth is, stay true to yourself. BUT BE A GOOD PERSON WHILE YOU'RE AT IT.

99

Gillian Anderson, actor

When the
heart is right,
the mind and
body will follow.

Coretta Scott King, author

"

You are beautiful,
EMBRACE IT;
you are intelligent,
EMBRACE IT;
you are powerful,
EMBRACE IT.

"

Michaela Coel,
actor and screenwriter

66

The minute you learn to love yourself, you won't want to be anyone else.

99

Rihanna, singer

66

I taught myself confidence. When I'd walk into a room and feel scared to death, I'd tell myself, 'I'm not afraid of anybody.' And people believed me. You've got to teach yourself to take over the world.

99

Priyanka Chopra, actor

"

Remember that first impressions are not always correct. You must always have faith in people. And, most importantly, you must always have faith in yourself.

"

Elle Woods, *Legally Blonde* (2001)

66

Focus on what matters. Honour your values and make decisions that are aligned with them.

99

Domonique Bertolucci, author

"

... when people try to tell you who you are, don't believe them. **YOU ARE THE ONLY CUSTODIAN OF YOUR OWN INTEGRITY,** and the assumptions made by those that misunderstand who you are and what you stand for reveal a great deal about them and absolutely nothing about you.

"

Maria Popova, writer

"

I wanted to be an independent woman, a woman who could pay for her bills, a woman who could run her own life – and I became that woman.

"

Diane von Furstenberg, fashion designer

**KNOW YOURSELF.
ACCEPT YOURSELF FOR WHO
YOU ARE, RIGHT WHERE YOU ARE.
And then create some boundaries
in your routine that aren't serving
you today in order to get closer to
the life and work you truly desire.**

Mel Robbins, lawyer

Making the decision to not follow a system, or someone else's rules has allowed me to really dig into what my own strengths and gifts are without spending time feeling jaded or wasteful.

Ishita Gupta,
founder of *Fear.less* magazine

66

BE THAT STRONG GIRL THAT EVERYONE KNEW WOULD MAKE IT THROUGH THE WORST,

be that fearless girl, the one who would dare to do anything, be that independent girl who didn't need a man; be that girl who never backed down.

99

Taylor Swift, singer

"

I figure, if a girl wants to be a **LEGEND**, she should go ahead and be one.

"

Cynthia Hand, *My Calamity Jane* (2020)

ENJOY
THE RIDE

With challenges and success come growth. Here are some ways to enjoy the ups and downs of your path's journey towards your goals, and to have resilience and determination to keep your dreams alive, no matter how bumpy the road ahead.

66

You will stumble and fall, you will experience both disaster and triumph, sometimes in the same day. But it's really important to remember that, like a hangover, neither triumphs nor disasters last forever.

99

Helen Mirren, actor

BELIEVE
you can
and you're
HALFWAY
THERE

" LIFE IS ABOUT CHANGE.

Sometimes it's painful.
Sometimes it's beautiful.
But most of the time,
it's both.

"

Lana Lang, *Smallville*

66

Change can be scary, but you know what's scarier? Allowing fear to stop you from growing, evolving, and progressing.

99

Mandy Hale, author

Now is the time to consider all the infinite possibilities with introspection, deliberation and thoughtfulness. Visualize the road ahead. Think about what excites you, what really gets your engine going. Engage in some real soul searching. Take a good, hard look at your strengths and weaknesses. A fulfilling professional life can be found at the intersection of what you love and what you're good at. And when you think you've discovered it, go at it full throttle.

Katie Couric, broadcaster

"

FEET, WHAT DO I NEED YOU FOR WHEN I HAVE WINGS TO FLY?

"

Frida Kahlo, artist

If you believe in something, don't ever give up. If one door closes, find a window to climb through. Surround yourself with loyal people who are good at doing the things you are not. Failure does not mean defeat. You have to be able to get back up again and learn and grow from your mistakes.

Bobbi Brown,
Women on TOPP, August 2022

Fall seven times

STAND UP EIGHT

"

If you're not making some notable mistakes along the way, you're certainly not taking enough business and career chances.

"

Sallie Krawcheck,
CEO and co-founder of Ellevest

66 Every twist and turn in life is an opportunity **to learn**

something new about yourself,

your interests, your talents, and

how to set and then achieve goals.

99

Jameela Jamil, actor

66

Give the world the BEST you have, and the BEST will come to you.

99

Madeline Bridges, poet

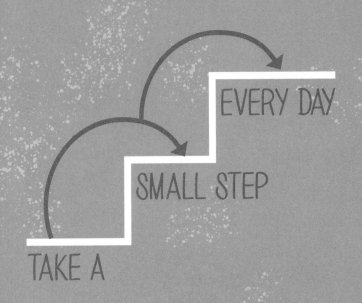

You may not control all
the events that happen to
you, but you can decide
not to be reduced by them.

Maya Angelou, poet

"

DO NOT BE AFRAID
to make decisions.
DO NOT BE AFRAID
to make mistakes.

"

Carly Fiorina,
former CEO of Hewlett-Packard

66

We need to accept that we don't always make the right decisions, that we'll screw up royally sometimes. Understand that failure is not the opposite of success, it's part of success.

99

Arianna Huffington,
founder of *Huffington Post*
and CEO of Thrive Global

THERE
ARE SECRET
OPPORTUNITIES
HIDDEN INSIDE
EVERY FAILURE.

" "

If we wait until we're ready, we'll be waiting for the rest of our lives. **LET'S GO.**

" "

Violet Baudelaire, *The Ersatz Elevator* (2001)

66

There's something liberating about not pretending. Dare to EMBARRASS YOURSELF. RISK.

99

Helen Mirren, actor

66

Live with intention.
Walk to the edge.
Listen Hard.
Practice wellness.
Play with abandon.
Laugh.
Choose with no regret.
Appreciate your friends.
Continue to learn.
Do what you love.
Live as if this is all there is.

99

Mary Anne Radmacher, author

"

She does not know
what the future holds,
but she is grateful for
**slow
and steady
growth.**

"

Morgan Harper Nichols, poet

There is nothing like a concrete life plan to weigh you down. Because if you always have one eye on some future goal, you stop paying attention to the job at hand, miss opportunities that might arise, and stay fixedly on one path, even when a better, newer course might have opened up.

Indra K. Nooyi, businesswoman

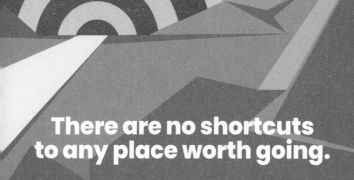

There are no shortcuts to any place worth going.

Beverly Sills, opera singer

"

I am not afraid of storms for I am learning how to sail my ship.

"

Louisa May Alcott, author

66

Life is ten per cent what you experience and ninety per cent how you respond to it.

99

Dorothy M. Neddermeyer, author

"

Bite off
more than
you can chew
THEN.
CHEW IT.

"

Ella Williams, surfer

Make time to

Celebrate

YOUR

Accomplishments

No matter how

BIG

or small

*

"

*Security is mostly
a superstition. Life
is either a daring
adventure or nothing.*

"

Helen Keller, disability advocate

66

A vision is not just a picture of what could be; it is an appeal to our better selves, a call to become something more.

99

Rosabeth Moss Kanter, professor of business at Harvard Business School

66

Never underestimate the power of dreams and the influence of the human spirit. We are all the same in this notion: The potential for greatness lives within each of us.

99

Wilma Rudolph, Olympic sprinter

Courage doesn't always roar. Sometimes courage is the little voice at the end of the day that says I'll try again tomorrow.

Mary Anne Radmacher,
writer and artist

"

If it's a good idea, go ahead and do it. It's much easier to apologize than it is to get permission.

"

Grace Hopper, computer scientist and US Navy rear admiral

66

WE'RE AMERICANS.
WE CELEBRATE SUCCESS.
We just don't want the
game to be rigged.

99

Elizabeth Warren, politician

66

The most important journey of our lives doesn't necessarily involve climbing the highest peak or trekking around the world. The biggest adventure you can ever take is to live the LIFE OF YOUR DREAMS.

99

Oprah Winfrey

**I don't focus on
what I'm up against.
I FOCUS
ON MY GOALS
and I try to ignore the rest.**

Venus Williams, tennis player

IF THE PLAN DOESN'T WORK, CHANGE THE PLAN, NOT THE GOAL.